How I Quit Drinking Alcohol Without Group Therapy

Don Moore

DEDICATIONS

To Pam, the love of my life.

CONTENTS

ACKNOWLEDGMENTS

For the courage He gave me when I prayed for it, I thank God.

For the love, trust and support I have received from her over the years, I thank my dear wife.

For all the love and trust they gave me over the years, I thank my wonderful children.

For helping when others had given up on me, I thank:

Georgia Doyle, DO

William H. Houston III, MD

Melissa M. Stockham, J.D., M.A.C.P., contributed far more to this book than she knows. Thank you again.

Joseph N. Moore deserves a special thanks for his tremendous formatting effort and cover design.

FOREWORD

IT'S NOT THAT BAD

If you bought this book for yourself, you are probably concerned that you have a drinking problem. If a friend or family member gave you this book, that person has serious concerns for you and has reached out to you. If your boss gave you this book, you may have real problems at work and do not realize it.

I feel certain that you can quit drinking and stay quit if you have the desire to quit. There is no doubt in my mind you can quit and be happy without alcohol. Quitting alcohol is not as difficult as you may fear. If I can quit forever and live happily around my family and friends who still drink, so can you.

In the first part of this book I will tell you the person I was before I quit drinking. I will tell you some really bad stuff about what I did when I was drunk. Trust me, I knew how to party. Then I will tell you how I quit drinking and how I stay totally alcohol free. You may recognize yourself in the first few chapters.

The next part of the book discusses what I feel you need to do to free yourself of alcohol and be happy with your life adjustment. Yours will be a personal program and not open to public scrutiny or critique. You will be the person most responsible for your accomplishments. You will monitor yourself and privately grade yourself on your level of success each day. We will simply discuss what you need to do to quit and get on with your life without alcohol. I am living proof that my plan works.

I tried group therapy twice and failed miserably because I had trouble exposing my innermost thoughts to people I did not know. I felt much more comfortable discussing my shortcomings in a dimly lit bar. I thought the people there would probably forget what I said by the next morning anyway. That sounds silly, but in my case it was true.

I knew I had to find a way to dry out and stay that way without a lot of unnecessary people involved in my pursuit of sobriety, telling me what I was doing wrong. I knew better than anyone when and where I was failing. I had to find my own way and stay with it.

This book will not require that you appear on morning television and admit to things you have done while you were drunk. You will not have to confess anything to anyone unless you so choose. Your opinion of yourself is the only opinion that matters. There may be people in your life who would be very hurt if they knew the complete story of your life under the influence of alcohol. Everyone concerned about you might live a happier life if all the details remain within you as motivation to help you stay away from alcohol.

I still socialize. I still go to college football games and parties with my family and friends. I go to the same bars with the same people as in the past, but I just do not drink alcohol anymore. You will see how I did it and how you too can quit drinking. There will be no hard sell and no magic potions.

3

I have been diagnosed with cirrhosis of the liver. It is a direct result of consuming too much alcohol over several years. Stopping any alcohol consumption and doing the things I discuss in this book have completely slowed the progression of the disease for over seven years. My doctors are amazed at my success. I hope that by going into detail regarding my personal history with alcohol and how I helped myself, you can see how the symptoms of problem drinking can creep into your own life.

If you drink more than three alcoholic beverages every day or drink enough to get drunk every day, you need to know what alcohol is doing to your body and mind. I learned a lot in a very short time to help me stay alive, and I share that information in this book.

There is hope within these pages. If you have been diagnosed with liver disease or if you think you may have a problem, there is information here that may be helpful to you. If you have been told by a physician that you have abnormal liver test results but no damage is visible on scans, there is information here that could help you avoid future problems.

I will describe symptoms of liver problems you can watch for on your body and in your body functions. You may not have been aware that these changes are actually signs that you are developing complications due to alcohol abuse. You need to know which blood tests do show liver problems and which ones do not. You need to know what is going on in your body, especially if you are still drinking alcohol.

I am not a doctor or a psychologist. The information I have provided about liver disease and pancreas problems comes from doctor visits, the internet and people I have talked with who have serious alcohol related health problems. If you are not sick and you plan to continue drinking regularly, you need to know how to help keep yourself as healthy as possible.

Do not use the information in this book as a treatment guide. I am telling you what I have witnessed, what I have been told and what I have read on the subject. If you have any concerns whatsoever that you may have a problem as a result of alcohol consumption, please seek medical attention as soon as possible. I cannot say that enough. Please see a doctor soon and do what the doctor tells you.

You may already have a health problem and do not know it. Until the day I found out I was sick and changed the direction of my life, I told myself that I did not have a problem and ignored what I now know were textbook symptoms of liver disease.

This book promotes a self-directed, self-motivated and self-managed approach to giving up alcohol altogether. I will attempt to show you how to find your personal direction and personal motivation to help you quit drinking forever and be happy about it. It is not a long book and I hope it is easy to read.

I will repeat myself several times in this book, and for a very good reason. I know from personal experience that some people read books about alcohol abuse while they are still abusing alcohol. Perhaps you are still drinking as you read this and might need a little refreshment of memory the next time you pick up the book. I sincerely hope that you will not be drinking alcohol when you finish the final chapter.

Thank you for opening this book. Hopefully, this will not be as painful as you think. Please keep reading.

CHAPTER ONE

HOW I BECAME WHO I WAS

Just before my 25th birthday, a small manufacturing company hired me to fill a clerical position assisting the company's production department in locating material and supplies they needed to complete day to day work schedules. I worked hard every day and attended college at night with financial help from the GI Bill. Our daughter attended day care so my wife could work as a secretary.

During the first five years of my employment at this young and growing company, key people took notice of my work ethic and my desire to complete my education. After my college graduation, upper management decided to send me to an Industrial Psychologist where I would be evaluated for possible promotions. I was given a full range of testing and an interview with a psychologist. The results showed I was ready to assume a more responsible position within the company and had the potential to become the company's first Marketing Manager.

Within weeks of my graduation, my wife gave birth to our son. We decided she should not go back to work because we felt very confident that my job was secure and my career path was upward. I had been told I was about to be promoted and given a handsome raise because I was considered an asset to my company. We were very pleased with every aspect of our lives.

Our company did not have a dedicated marketing team. Our estimating and management staff talked with the existing accounts and new customers found us through word of mouth within the industry. The decision was made to create a sales department and I was chosen to go out and locate new customers. I had an unlimited travel budget, a new title and a one way ticket to the penthouse.

With extreme luck and lots of hard work, I was successful from the very beginning. The man assigned as my boss already managed two other departments, so I had a great amount of freedom to seek out new customers. One sales call per day was sufficient, considering each sale could easily be worth at least $100,000.00. I would fly to New York for lunch and fly home the same day so I could be in the office the next morning. My time was becoming very valuable and I was having a great time.

I was locating the potential customers and calling for appointments with absolutely no fear of rejection. Many of the people I called on had never heard of us. I was making cold calls and turning them into friends. I was spending a considerable amount of time entertaining my new friends on the company's money and we were being rewarded with a considerable amount of new business. I loved every minute of this new success and freedom. The good people back at the office were handling the work while I hung out in really nice bars with interesting people who were making us lots of money.

My young family was becoming a sales tool when our new customers were in town. We lived very near my place of business, so I would frequently invite my customers to our home for meals or cocktails after work. My wife always made them feel welcome and prepared home cooked meals for them. We kept their brands of liquor, wine or beer at our home so they would feel even more at home. We would eat and drink into the night, as if the customers were family visiting from out of town. Several clients would send our children gifts for their birthdays and Christmas.

Many of my customers were from the old school where "drinking lunch" was a way of life. When we had active contracts being accomplished at our facility, we worked hard from daylight until lunch. Then we would find a place to eat, drink beer and discuss the jobs our workers were to perform the rest of the day while we were on the golf course. There were many times I would come home drunk by three in the afternoon. My company thought that drinking with the customers was part of my job description, so my short days were expected and even applauded. I occupied the customer's time so production could work without interruption.

GROWING PAINS

Within a few years of my move to sales, we began to experience growing pains. The founder of our company decided that we needed outside management consultants to show us how we could continue to grow and become even more successful. I was usually on the road, so I was not a part of the management decisions being made as to the future of the company. I was concerned only with making large amounts of money for myself, my family and the company. I assumed everything else would take care of itself.

The management consultants convinced upper management that we needed to add more sales people. If we could grow this fast with one salesman, we could grow much faster with more sales people doing the same job in other areas. I had no problem with that possibility because I already knew the company from top to bottom and they planned to bring in professional sales people from outside the company. I knew the product and the incoming people would have to take the time to learn everything I already knew.

The new sales people wanted to be successful and therefore wanted to absorb some of my customers. I did not have to resist because the customers did it for me. They already had a marketing man they liked who would act as their intercessor when they had contracts with our company. They were receiving value for their money and enjoying the relationship with me and my family. We would drink and play golf most of the day while the work was being done on time and at a fair price. Many of the customers insisted I stay as their account representative and, one by one, the new salesmen resigned or were terminated.

PARTY HERE, PARTY THERE

I felt that I was placing too much of a burden on my wife, so we tried to find something that we both enjoyed that would be fun to do together when I was home. We had fun with our kids, did PTA, T-ball, camping and many other activities as a family in our motor home. Still, I felt that the two of us should have time together with other grown ups and be able to enjoy ourselves away from work and customers.

My wife loves to dance, so we started taking dance lessons for country and western two-step music and line dancing. We did that type of dancing for a few years and decided that beach music dance lessons would also be fun. We became quite accomplished at beach music dancing and really enjoyed the parties that were a part of the beach music culture. Dancing became a large part of our already busy life.

We would dance at least twice each week when I was in town. We would get in the bar around happy hour for lessons during the week and leave at a fairly reasonable hour so I could go to work the next day. On several occasions, Friday nights became the beginning of a two night dance party weekend. We would dance until the bars closed and then go to an all night café for breakfast with our fellow dancers so we could all sober up enough to drive home.

We would spend time with the kids on Saturdays and quite often go back to one of the beach bars on Saturday nights to meet our dance group. These bars really enjoyed my wife and I being there because we were the life of the party and I always had the biggest bar tab of the group. My wife drank quite a bit less than I did and danced considerably more than me because I have absolutely no rhythm. I would spend quite a bit of time at "our" table in the dance club, buying this one or that one a drink to make sure everyone had a good time and watch my wife line dance or dance with other guys. She always saved the slow dances for me.

Many times during our dance club days, I was traveling during the week and flying back home on Friday nights. There were many occasions when my wife would pick me up at the airport and we would drive directly to the dance club. I had no problem at all with this lifestyle because I was with my wife and away from the stress of my job. When the dancing was over for the weekend, it was time to get back on the road and entertain the customers for another week.

BIG SUCCESS

BIGGER PROBLEMS

I wanted it all and the company was willing to accommodate me. I told management that we did not need to retry the experiment and hire different salesmen. Just make the box bigger and I would keep it filled. I was raking in the money and my ego was totally off the charts.

While I was flying around the world making deals, my fellow employees were back at the plant making modest but steady gains in their positions and in their influence with the ownership. I could care less because I was out in the market making things happen. I was later told they were back at the plant making the same point over and over to the owner that the real reason for our success was because we had such a great company as a whole and I was easily replaceable. I was too self consumed and maybe too naïve to see this going on or to see it as a problem for me.

After a few years of trying to keep up this pace and maintain the same level of growth, I began to have panic attacks during meetings and on airplanes. My heart would pound uncontrollably when I drove over a long or high bridge. My doctor prescribed anti-anxiety medication and suggested I take the full dosage only if I needed it. I would adjust my dosage to match what I felt my level of stress would be for that day.

After a few months, I was taking a whole tablet every day. When I was on the road, I would supplement the medication with wine at lunch, good whiskey before dinner and a fine wine to compliment the entrée. I did not tell anyone at work of my problems and I kept most of this bad news from my wife.

After a few more years, my fear of flying was almost unbearable. Bad weather was always a problem, but I was becoming afraid to fly on sunny days. Instead of flying across country for lunch and back home that night, I was flying out in the evening so I could take a full dosage of the anti-anxiety medication and a blood pressure pill so I would have the courage to board the plane. I would also self medicate with good whiskey before and during the flight. I would still be shaking when I arrived at my destination. Looking back, I wonder if I was afraid of the flight or that I might fail when I arrived at my destination.

Our friends were beginning to notice a difference in me. One of my friends in the dance club asked if I should ease up on my travel schedule or maybe hire some help. I laughed at the suggestion because I remembered all those sales people who were now employed elsewhere. I knew I was becoming a basket case, but I hoped I could pull myself out of this dive.

My personal career situation continued to deteriorate during the next several years. The level of cooperation I had been receiving was rapidly decreasing. As situations in my work place grew more worrisome, my fear of going into meetings became even more intense. I was having chest pains, shortness of breath and a real fear of dying on the road. I began to panic during meetings so badly that on occasion I would want to run out of the room.

I was in trouble and I knew it. I just did not know how I could escape the situation. I would count the hours and minutes until I could start happy hour. I would build my sales days around having lunch with good customers who were still day drinkers. I sure was, because I needed a drink by lunchtime.

PICK ONLY THE PRETTIEST FLOWERS

Due to the size of our company, losing a sizeable bid job could mean that many of the hourly employees would be laid off their jobs. They would be out of work until I found other profitable business for the company. I knew most of the workers by name and my kids went to school with their kids, so I took every lay off very personally.

Many of the hourly workers had cheered when I was promoted and took pride that one of their own was reaching a top level with the company. During slow work periods I was never in town. I would be out in the market contacting every potential customer possible in hopes of finding profitable business that would make everyone happy and keep all the workers employed.

Management was growing financially fat and my influence was beginning to wane. We had become so accustomed to high gross profit work that average profits were unacceptable. On one side I had management telling me that I could not take work for less than X, but our competitors were catching up with us on price and quality. On the other side, I had all these workers who would be out of work if I failed, and my personal incentive pay was based on gross profit. I had to sell the work at a good profit or my company would want to know what I was doing wrong.

I was almost living on the road, trying to keep my company full of profitable work. I would usually leave early Tuesday and return Friday night or Saturday morning. On several occasions, I actually got down on my knees in my hotel room and prayed that I could sell work the next day. If I failed to close a big job, I would sometimes cry myself to sleep in the hotel room. I was now closing the day with good whiskey and counting the minutes until I met my lunch partner for drinks.

When I called the office to ask if we could adjust numbers on items, I was being- second guessed as to why I needed to get help on pricing. I had sold the same work at that price before, so what was I doing wrong now? On most occasions, I was told I needed to try harder with the same prices.

My family was having real problems with my actions. I would fly back home on Fridays and arrive at the airport so drunk that my wife would have to drive me home. I was relieved to have a few days with people I loved but my family was becoming less excited about my trips home. All I wanted to do was drink and sleep unless we went dancing, where I would be drinking anyway. My family was now entertaining our customers while I was on the road in search of more business. My kids knew I was under stress, but they felt that they also deserved some happy time with me. I was too mentally and physically exhausted to share much in their lives anymore and I had to get some rest to prepare for the next week of traveling.

THE PARTY'S OVER

I was fired the easy way. After almost thirty years in the business, my employment contract was not renewed. I was told the company had decided to go in a different direction. I was packed and gone within a few minutes. Just like that, it was over. The stress, the worry, and the demands on me and my family were gone. We were so relieved when it was over that my wife and I actually cried for joy. We would have to make some financial adjustments, but we knew that we would be just fine without the stress we had endured as a family.

Looking back, I voluntarily put myself in a position to absorb large amounts of stress in order to make large amounts of money for myself, my family and my company. I had endured incredible stress and I used it as an excuse to justify my drinking habits. I used alcohol as a marketing tool in the beginning, but I now feel I began to abuse that same tool until it almost destroyed my physical and personal life as well as my career.

CHAPTER TWO

SO MUCH BOOZE, SO LITTLE TIME

I received a generous financial settlement. My former employer had a non-participating profit sharing program that would help set up my retirement. We had also bought stock in the company when it was cheap and sold at a good profit when I left. I was not worried about money and I was actually happy that I was out of my former situation. I was positive that the stress I endured was because of the management team of my former company and had nothing to do with my drinking habits.

I was only 55 years old, so I intended to get right back to work in the same market. I would prove to my former employer that I was the major reason for the success we had enjoyed over the years. However, my wife and I decided I should take some time off before I began my new job search. We would enjoy a few months of freedom and then begin reconstructing my career.

The next several months were a blur of early lunches at restaurants that featured two for one well drinks and lunch specials. As I said, we were trying to economize. My wife is not much of a day drinker, so I was going home after lunch with at least three vodka and club sodas under my belt. A long nap usually followed and I would get up just in time for happy hour by our pool. After one or two bottles of wine and a small meal I was happily off to bed. Thanks to the loving efforts of my wife and children, I was really enjoying myself.

Actually, I was not consuming much more alcohol than I did when I was working and I was beginning to enjoy nap time. Our kids were grown and out of the house so my wife and I ate, drank and slept when we chose. We were on a very nice vacation at our own home.

My wife was trying to allow me to recover from my years of trying to please everyone so she wanted me to please myself for a change. However, I was beginning to become an embarrassment in my pursuit of a stress free life. After way too much wine one night, I fell in front of some friends. I jumped to my feet and proudly proclaimed that I did not spill a single drop of wine. I emptied the glass and fell again. My wife told everyone that I had taken quite a bit of pain medication for the osteoarthritis I suffer with, which was true, and the medicine was not mixing well with the wine. We said our goodbyes and my wife drove us home. I staggered into our house and fell into bed.

GUESS HOW SICK I AM

I was falling quite a bit the next few months. I had a middle ear infection on two occasions a few years earlier so I went to my doctor, who remembered the ear problems and gave me medicine to treat vertigo. My wife and I did not mention that I was dizzy because I was consuming huge amounts of alcohol on a daily basis and had been for years. The medication only made me want to sleep that much more.

On a routine visit to obtain more anti-anxiety medication and blood pressure refills, my primary physician noted I had not had any blood tests in a few years. She wrote prescriptions for the drugs and also wrote orders for blood tests. I filled the prescriptions and put the lab orders in my glove box. I knew that if I had blood work done I might be told to stop drinking, but I did not want to stop during football season. I was afraid something might be wrong, but I wasn't ready to admit it. My eyes were clear and my skin was tanned. I looked like the picture of health.

I started writing my resume and meeting with old business acquaintances. We would drink our lunch and discuss job possibilities. About this time, I started to notice that my forearms were itching almost every day after I had lunch. I decided to stop having vodka for lunch and instead have the wine specials. This wasn't helping, so I made an appointment with my doctor's office.

I asked for an appointment with a physician's assistant in my doctor's office who did not concern herself with the fact I had not had recent lab tests. This was good, I thought. No hassles, just cure the itch. She gave me prescriptions for salve and an oral medication. The PA asked me if I consumed more than three alcoholic beverages per day. I laughed and asked her if there was a retiree she knew who did not. She laughed and told me that I should not drink while I took the medication. I told her that was not a problem. I filled the prescription for the salve and placed the prescription for the oral antibiotic in my glove box.

The itching was actually the result of my body's bile products being dumped into my skin tissues. The bile products could not follow its normal path to my liver because of the damage already present. This is a definite symptom of liver disease, but I was ignorant of the possibility I was very sick. I would not discuss my alcohol consumption with my PA because I was sure that she would push for blood tests. I was itching but I was also having too much fun to stop what I was doing.

My feet began to swell and my pulse was increasing at an alarming rate. I went back to the PA. She gave me a prescription for a harsh diuretic. One of the side effects of the medicine was that my breasts could enlarge. I knew I needed relief, so I took the chance and filled the prescription.

I started passing a considerable amount of water and my ankles began to reduce in size. I was not surprised I was retaining water because I was consuming much more beer and wine to compensate for the loss of the vodka lunches. The only problem was my breasts were beginning to hurt and feel as if they were growing. My PA also thought that the diuretic was the cause of the growth and switched my medications. None of us realized that my breasts were growing as a complication of liver disease.

I had been semi-retired a total of nine months and I was not feeling well at all. I was having trouble with my balance, my feet were swelling and I was itching all the time. I was also getting fat around the middle. I just did not feel well. I was sleeping too much and I could not remember half the things I was supposed to pick up at the grocery store.

I started noticing that my skin color had started to look a little different. I did not know if I was spending too much time in the sun or not enough. My eyes were also starting to look yellow and they were almost always puffy. I thought that was because I stayed up late playing on the computer and drinking, so I just let it go and did not mention the issue to anyone.

NO MORE GAMES

Finally, my wife said she enough was enough. She called my doctor's office to make an appointment and told the receptionist I would not be see by a PA. She insisted that I have an appointment with my physician and she wanted the appointment for that day.

My doctor walked into the examining room, took one look at me and began ordering tests. My wife and my doctor were now doing all the talking. I was the subject and not a participant in the conversation. My opinions were not welcome in this discussion. My doctor looked me in the eyes and asked "What have you done to yourself?"

The doctor told me to lie down on the examining table. She went directly to my abdomen to begin an external examination. She told us that most of the health problems I had mentioned to the PA would have been looked at much differently if I had only admitted that I had consumed large amounts of alcohol for a long period of time. Blood tests were ordered. Liver tests such as AST, ALT and bilirubin were specified. Sonograms of my abdomen were scheduled. An appointment with a liver specialist was scheduled for after the test results were confirmed.

We were about to find out how alcohol and my ignorance of its effects had damaged my body. I really did not want to know the answers because I was afraid of the consequences. I knew I would be forced into some life altering situations if the results came back the way I feared they would.

For the first time in a very long time, I went home and went to bed completely sober. I desperately wanted something to drink, but I knew my wife would go nuts if I had just one beer. I was thinking, OK, here it comes. Thirty-odd years of drinking had finally caught up with me and it was time to stand up straight and take my medicine.

CHAPTER THREE

BAD NEWS

The liver specialist told me and my wife that all the tests showed that I had cirrhosis of the liver. He told us I was very sick. I knew I was sick, but I thought that I would take the cure for a few months and then I would be right back at the party. My doctor told me I had to quit drinking forever. I said I would, but not one of us in the room believed a word of it.

My wife and I struggled with the fact that I had the worst possible scenario that could happen to people who drink to excess. We asked the doctor if he was sure of the diagnosis. He said there was no doubt I had cirrhosis. He calmly looked at both of us and solemnly told me that I only had between four months and four years to live. He said the two determining factors as to

31

how long I survived were how badly my liver was damaged and if I could stay away from alcohol altogether. In other words, I could quit and feel better or keep drinking and quickly lose my life.

The doctor told us the liver takes years of abuse before it is severely damaged, but when it does start to fail it deteriorates faster with continued abuse. He told us the liver does not hurt you when you abuse it. It just gets worse and worse. Lesions begin to form and then you are really sick. This was not good news.

The doctor stood up and gathered his papers to leave the conference room, but he did not offer his hand. He looked at me with a sad look on his face, said that he was truly sorry. He said he was sorry for me and told me to make a follow-up appointment with my primary physician. I asked if there was any medication he could give me to help immediately. He just looked at me with those sad eyes and slowly shook his head. I didn't know if I was angry at him or scared. Oh, I knew. I was too scared to be mad at anyone.

We left the building in silence and only looked at one another in glances. I thought, I am such an idiot. I had waited too long to quit. Why didn't I quit years earlier when I first had abnormal liver test results? And now, I'm going to die an ugly death because I wouldn't quit drinking. What an absolute idiot.

We did not talk a lot on the way home because I did not know what to say. I had made some really bad life choices in that I knew I had problems and chose to ignore the obvious. I knew I had a drinking problem, but most of my business associates did, too. That was my justification in the past, but it was not working this time. All I could think was, damn, I have really done it this time. I had broken my wife's heart and I had absolutely no other person in the whole world to blame but myself.

I knew I had been wrong to ignore the warning signs, but I did not know my body was presenting obvious symptoms of a life threatening disease. I was unaware of the ultimate consequences of too many nights of too much whiskey. For the moment I was trying to block out what I had just heard from a trained and licensed liver specialist. This just could not be real.

Our visit to my primary physician turned into her closing arguments as to why I was very sick and why my illness was not her fault. Malpractice was never mentioned, but the words from her mouth were attorney words and not doctor words. It was very obvious to me and my wife the doctor was more concerned about her practice than she was about my well being.

We wished her well and left her office for the last time. I was very sick and I had just been fired by my doctor. We accepted the situation and started making plans to move forward. I was not thinking about a drink that day. I was trying to figure out how to live for longer than four months.

SECOND OPINIONS

My wife said that I needed a fresh start with doctors who had positive attitudes and experience with liver disease. She said maybe a positive outlook from my doctors would improve our attitudes as well. I was still trying to fully accept the fact that I was very sick and I was ready to try anything that would make me better or maybe even well.

The time for fooling around with my health was over. A friend of ours had a primary physician she thought was great and we decided to give this doctor a call. She was an older lady who cut to the chase when telling patients what they had to do to get healthy. I feel that constructive criticism is one of the most positive responses you can get from someone, so I was excited about this lady as soon as I met her.

This new doctor had an air of confidence that made me feel as if I was finally in competent and caring hands. I was very impressed with her total approach to medicine and asked her if she would please help me and be my new doctor. She said she would if I agreed to stay sober and work toward becoming as healthy as possible. My new doctor gave us hope that I might be healthy once again. We knew I would never be the same as before, but at least I could be alive and be with my family.

My new doctor conducted her own examination of my abdomen and ordered some additional tests. After she received the new test results, she confirmed my original doctor's diagnosis. However, she said that if I did not drink and followed her instructions I could very possibly extend my lifespan. I was placed on a regimen of good quality vitamins with an emphasis on B-complex and folic acid to compliment my new medication. I had gone about two weeks with nothing to drink. My wife was also monitoring every step I made. I was not a prisoner but I was being very closely watched.

My doctor recommended a liver specialty clinic in our town that is well known throughout the medical community. Her referral group called for an appointment but was told the clinic was not accepting any new patients who were already diagnosed with liver disease. My wife was so determined I would be seen by one their specialists she called the specialist's office and begged for an appointment. She actually had to plead with the office manager to secure an appointment for me.

The liver specialist assigned as my doctor was obviously very knowledgeable, but he always acted as if he was angry with me. I knew I had to accept the punishment to obtain help in my quest to live. I agreed to cooperate with him and do whatever he said to stop the progression of cirrhosis. I secretly hoped I was not misleading him and everyone else who was trying to help me.

I had heard the Veterans Administration was very good at working with people who have alcohol related illnesses, so we decided to seek help there as well. I applied for medical benefits based upon my honorable wartime service and was mailed an appointment letter. I was not expecting much as far as skilled people at the VA, but to my amazement I was assigned to a physician who is a real gentleman and a great doctor.

He has always shown respect for me and a genuine concern for my wellbeing. He prescribed the right medications to help stabilize my blood pressure, pulse and liver functions as much as possible. He manages my long term care and encourages me at each visit. He has helped me understand what my condition is all about and what we need to do to make me as healthy as possible for a long time. My copays are a bargain considering the quality of care I am receiving from the VA.

I will forever sing the praises of the entire VA system. Veterans are treated with respect by virtually everyone employed in the system. Qualified veterans pay for all or part of their care based upon their ability to pay. Considering the huge number of patients they serve, I am absolutely amazed at the high quality of care offered to America's veterans by the VA. In my opinion, this is taxpayer money very well spent.

HEY, WAIT A MINUTE

The new liver specialist set up some additional blood tests for a few days after my initial visit. I left my house early one morning and drove to the lab to give a blood sample. On the way over to the lab and while I waited for my name to be called, I pondered my past and future. How can I find it within myself to give up something I have enjoyed doing for thirty-odd years? I will not go back to group therapy again. I am done with that. So how can I make this happen? How can I fix this situation so I do not embarrass my family ever again? How can I live without alcohol? What do I tell my kids, the rest of my family and my close friends?

The lab finished with me and I drove away, still trying to come up with a real plan of action. I drove around awhile until my wife called on my cell phone. She wanted to know if I had finished at the lab and when I would be home. I told her I was on my way home, but I took the long way to give myself a little more time alone. I drove around the same neighborhood for another half hour or so.

And that very moment, I got it. It was just like algebra in the ninth grade. I did not understand algebra at all, and I was sure I was going to fail and be a bum for the rest of my life. As I sat in class with all this incredible self doubt and uncertainty, my teacher drew out on the blackboard for the ninety-second time how X plus Y times something gives you the right number and this is why it works. And there it was. I got it. Suddenly, I was passing algebra and moving on to the next level. That was exactly how it happened again that morning when I opened my eyes.

I had to get mad at myself. I would make sure I stayed totally sober for the rest of my life or else. No person on earth could be as tough on me as I can. On two occasions I had gone to everyone I hold dear and apologized for my actions over the years as I tried to stay sober, and within a few weeks or months I was drinking again. I swore to myself that this time would be different. This time, I will do it myself.

I knew I had to look myself in the mirror every day and tell myself that if I messed up this time I was dead for real. I had to ask myself how in goodness did I let this go this far. If I even considered a drink I could go to a bathroom, look at myself in the eyes and say some hard words to this stupid idiot.

I would just quit drinking and act as my own enforcer. I can extend my own life and enjoy every minute as long as my mind absolutely refuses to allow my body to consume alcohol. Every time I see a bottle of booze, my mind must remember what I would lose if I take a drink. Not what I could lose, but what I would lose. If I take another drink, I have failed in my commitment to myself and my family. I had to get mad at myself and stay angry until I made alcohol irrelevant to my life.

I had to quit drinking alcohol forever. I knew I could do it if I guarded my own personal actions and constantly remembered what I had to lose if I failed. Everyone can drink all they want except me and that's the way it has to be for the rest of my life.

I was mad at myself for what I had done to my family, my friends and my own body. How could I have done this for so long and thought I could get away with it?

This was way past stupid. All I could do was shake my head in disbelief at my own idiotic actions. The more I thought about it, the madder I became.

There it was. Just accept the fact you will force yourself to stay sober for the rest of your life and then just leave alcohol alone. Alcohol would be all around me but I could never taste it again as long as I lived. That is not a bold statement when you say it to yourself and you are confident in your own mind that you can do it. You are the person making the promise to your own self and if you even think about a drink this angry person inside you will get very ugly. I sat there in my car and swore to myself that I had quit. I knew that alcohol was now irrelevant to my life.

I drove to my home with a quiet resolve. I now knew that I had quit. I walked into our house, quietly proud of myself. My wife followed me into our home office and asked how I was doing, and I told her I had finally quit drinking. She gave me a strange look and asked what in Heaven was I saying. I smiled and said "I have just quit drinking. I am angry at myself for what I have done and I am ready to quit." After a long look at my smiling face, she smiled back and understood.

IT'S GOING TO BE OK

We knew I was still very sick, but I was willing to give myself a fighting chance. Win or lose, I would live the rest of my life without alcohol. That was the least I owed my family. I will live sober until I die. Maybe I could live long enough to erase some of the hurtful memories from their minds.

We knew we were finally on the right track. I was listening to my new doctors and they knew it. They responded with high quality care and encouragement.

Even the crusty liver specialist was working on his attitude. I think that in the beginning he was not convinced I could really quit drinking and when I first met him I am not sure I was totally convinced.

IT'S A START

The medications and vitamins were starting to take effect in my body. I was beginning to build up enough strength to ride an exercise bike for thirty minutes every few days. I would have to take a short nap afterwards, but my doctor said that the exercise was vital to my recovery. Exercise became less of an effort until I was bicycling every day.

My family doctor told me to force down lots and lots of water. The diuretics would move all this water directly through me, but it had a strange smell and color as I passed it. I found out later that I was actually flushing my body of poisons and did not realize it. I guess my doctor was tired of explaining her methods and was just telling me to do this and do that. It was all working.

We were focused on doing what we were told to make me better and I was not even thinking about taking a drink of liquor. Liquor was there in my home and my wife would have a glass of wine with our friends, but I was not even considering alcohol for myself. I knew that angry person in my head would create havoc with my peace of mind if I even considered a drink. Our children were already becoming accustomed to seeing me sober. Just a few months had passed, but I was already starting to feel good and feel good about myself. My attitude was becoming more positive every day.

I had quit drinking and I was going to be healthy for a few years at least. To go back to drinking now would be a crime against my family. I knew there were still some issues to deal with in molding my new life to fit with everyone else, but I had quit drinking alcohol and I was determined to stay that way. There was no turning back.

CHAPTER FOUR

TIME TO CHANGE

Physically, I was doing much better. We were determined to get that part right and we were succeeding. We now had a great team of doctors and a very willing patient. That part was going well, but I had to look at my life structure to allow this new me to happily coexist with people I cared about an awful lot.

My wife and I had several long discussions about my habits and how they were interconnected to the use of alcohol. Almost everything I considered fun included the consumption of alcohol. The more fun I had at something, the greater the possibility was I would get drunk. Wine and dine, football and beer, cookouts and beer, early golf and a Bloody Mary or two from the thermos until the beer cart showed up; the list just went on and on. If I were to quit drinking altogether, I had to change my mind set regarding social activities and drinking.

OK, so I had quit. How do I fit the new me into my old world? Actually, how do I refit my world into theirs and keep everyone happy? Do I sit around the house all day and watch television? I do not watch TV a lot. Do I take up new hobbies that do not include anyone taking a drink around me? I could not consider that possibility.

Am I required to find an entirely new set of friends who do not drink? They are our friends and they did not create this problem. The idiot in the mirror caused the damage. Some of our existing friends have been known to get as drunk as I once did, but they were just not as frequently intoxicated as I was. Maybe that is why they are still drinking and I am not.

I had to accept that I would be sober no matter what was going on around me, or everyone else would have to change to accommodate me. Every person I know would have to know that to associate with me would mean a day or night of total sobriety because I had changed. My situation would have to be public knowledge. "He's a drunk and I will not sit around with a ginger ale just because he can't handle his drinking." There was no way I would ask anyone to do that.

I decided to think of what I did want and what I did not want. I definitely did not want everyone knowing the truth about my illness. That sounds silly, but I will not take pity from anyone. I am a very stubborn and proud person. I did not want my former employers to feel relieved that they had fired me at just the right time and avoided any long term liabilities. I did not want a single person to feel sorry for me. I would not give anyone the opportunity to shake their heads and say how sad it is that I could not control myself when it comes to alcohol.

DECISION TIME

I thought hard and prayed hard. I knew I would need my wife's help, But I also wanted and needed spiritual guidance. I definitely did not want my children or my friends to be involved in my recovery. They would all be part of my life but not a participant in my program to quit drinking alcohol. If I failed, I did not want anyone to live their lives thinking they had let me down by not being there all the time. I have seen people angry at themselves for a lifetime because they did not do what they thought was enough to help a friend or loved one. Only one person should be angry in this instance, and that is the guilty party.

My wife is a major player in my effort and should be given a large share of the credit for my success so far. If I fail tomorrow, it will be my fault. I will not use anyone or my religion as a crutch. One person put me in this situation and that person is me. I have to convince only one person that I must quit and that one person is me. I must answer to only one person if I fail, and that person is me. That is the bottom line to the whole story.

I swore to myself that from this time forward, I would work as hard as necessary to be as healthy as I can for as long as I can. I would live my life as happily as I could for as long as possible. Hopefully, I could live long enough and show enough love to my family that they would forget what I looked like when I was falling down drunk. I would eliminate alcohol consumption from my personal life, but not affect the lifestyles of anyone else.

I had been around alcohol the entire time since I found out that I needed to quit. At first, I did not pour out the liquor we had because I assumed I would just have to go back to the liquor store and buy more when I started drinking again. Opening a bottle of wine was a part of the ritual of sitting down for dinner. I will open a bottle for everyone else but me for the rest of my life. I simply cannot have what is in the bottle. I will not have what is in the bottle.

I do not brag that I have gone X number of days since my last drink. I do not tell stories of how stupid I was when I was drunk. People who have known me for a long time already know those stories because they have witnessed my behavior when I was under the influence of alcohol. Instead of refreshing everyone's memories as to how I was, I am now helping them forget by being their designated driver and enjoying my penance.

It is as if I quit smoking and lots of people still smoke around me. Ex-smokers can successfully mix with smokers. Reformed smokers find that the ones who still use tobacco smell of smoke, but they do not ban smokers from their lives as a rule. People who no longer drink alcohol can happily coexist with people who still drink. I am usually amused with people who have too much to drink and act the same way I did when I was under the influence of alcohol. I know that they will be mad at themselves tomorrow morning if they can remember what they did to make themselves feel so badly for a whole day.

After a few months, an amazing transformation began to happen. My family and friends stopped commenting that I was drinking non-alcohol beer at parties. It became a non-subject. It was simply accepted as fact that I did not drink alcoholic beverages. A few friends now buy my brand of NA beer for me and keep it at their homes in case we visit, the same way we buy a certain brand of whiskey or gin for other friends. Some of my friends now drink my beer on hot summer days. They say it is more refreshing than beer with alcohol and I truly feel they are right.

Friends we have made since I quit are not aware of the fact that I was a heavy drinker. They would have trouble imagining me drunk, falling on the way to my car. I am not afraid of alcohol. I am afraid of its effects on me and the effects it would have on me if I started back drinking.

TIME FOR ACTION

I am absolutely positive I will never, ever get drunk again as long as I live. No matter how healthy my liver gets, I am through with alcohol. I cannot do that to myself or my precious family ever, ever again. There would be four broken hearts and one of those would be mine. I will not allow myself to go back to my old ways because I would irreparably damage the family I helped build and rebuild. If medical science devised a cure for liver disease, I would not go back to being a functional drunk.

I do not have to say no to alcohol. It is there but I do not use it anymore. When I first got dry and sober, I would look at myself in the mirror every morning and congratulate myself on another day well done. I would make a plan for that day that did not include me drinking alcohol. If I was to be in a situation where people were drinking, I could look at it, smell it, and pour a drink for someone else. I would just absolutely refuse to allow myself to even consider the possibility of taking a drink.

Today, I do not even think about having a drink. I look at my face in the mirror and see an extra line or two. Eyebrows are getting a little thin, but my eyes are clear and alive. I made myself learn to ignore alcohol and it has worked. My strongest action has been no action whatsoever. I see it but I will not taste it again as long as I live and I do not mind in the least.

The best thing I did early on was to spend some time alone with myself and make peace between my mind and my body. I resolved within myself to do this thing once and forever. I did not consider failure as a possibility. I did not look at goals per se. I simply said that I was sober at that moment and I would not allow any problem or situation in my future to lead me back to drinking.

I swore to myself that this was it, and I would not let myself down ever again. I promised I would be true to myself. I promised me that I would stay sober and not allow any weakness I have to be a problem in anyone else's life ever again. It does not hurt to be sober.

Today, I know in my heart that I am sober and I will be until I die as an old man. When I was told how sick I was, living to be an old man was not even a consideration. I have made peace with myself and I am happy as a sober person.

RESULTS

I do not believe I could have quit by committee. However, if you feel you would benefit by external positive reinforcement, by all means go to group therapy sessions and see if they help you. Many people have benefited from that environment. I have tried group therapy twice, but it did not work for me. In order to stay sober and win the battle, this may be an additional path you need to follow. Use every round of ammunition available in your war against alcohol.

Using my approach to get away from alcohol, I feel terrific. I am years past the best survival date given to me at the beginning of this journey. Sounds corny even to me, but this truly has been a "journey" through my life as a changed man.

Sonograms and CT scans from years ago showed varices in my esophagus and ascites in my abdomen. Either malady could kill you. Recent tests show no visible varices and the ascites in my abdomen is gone (we will discuss these two maladies later in this book). I occasionally look at copies of the reports from years ago and the recent ones. They read as if two different people were examined.

I am currently in a physical stage my doctor calls "compensated cirrhosis." I stopped damaging my liver, gave it some nourishment and it has responded. I am told that if I begin drinking again the downward spiral will begin again at a rapid rate. The damage to my liver is obvious on my original CT scan, but it is not becoming worse at this time because I took the right steps at exactly the right moment.

I could not have been successful without the cooperation of my family, my doctors, my mind and my body. My prayers have been answered to allow me to be here today, telling you that you can do what I did and be just as successful as I am in this plan to quit drinking. I am not proud of many of the things I have done before I quit, but I am very proud of myself today.

I have lived the past few years with a new awareness and a revived appreciation of those close to me. Using my plan, I have quit drinking and stayed quit. I am happy and I believe my family feels the same way. I have found peace without alcohol.

CHAPTER FIVE

LOOK AT YOURSELF

We have gone from a book about me to a book about you. I had to tell you about where I was and where I am to find out where you are in your life with alcohol. Now, you need to figure out if you are ready and willing to give up alcohol and get started on the right path.

Here are some of the key ingredients to my formula for quitting alcohol. Some people may disagree with my philosophy and want to take a much more open effort to help you quit drinking. I am totally against that plan. I have myself and others to point to who have quietly made the transition from problem drinker to happy sober person.

* First and foremost, you must convince yourself that you will quit and stay quit. No other living person can

do that for you. Do not forget that. I cannot say that enough.

* Take it easy on yourself. You may have done some pretty bad things while you were under the influence. Your thinking was impaired. Now, you are taking the steps necessary to make things right.

* Never, ever refer to yourself as a drunk. If you call yourself a drunk, others will feel free to repeat that opinion. You got drunk, but you have quit drinking. Drunks cannot quit drinking. You can. You quit.

* Also, I will not refer to myself as an alcoholic. You may fit the definition, but you have quit drinking. You are no longer dependent on alcohol. You are no longer under the influence of alcohol. You were a heavy drinker, but you quit.

* Do not give up your pride. Be proud of your decision to give up alcohol. Even if you experience significant withdrawal symptoms, remember that this is the last time you will have to go through such torture. It may be painful for a short time, but it will be all right. Stay proud. You are doing the right thing. You are saving your own life. You are not a drunk. You quit.

NO SUBSTITUTIONS

You may not enjoy the first few days or weeks of living without alcohol. I surely did not. I mentioned earlier that I had a prescription for an anti-anxiety medication, but my new doctor told me that to be totally sober I had to also give up this drug. She told me I should continue taking smaller and smaller doses to wean myself from the drug. I was able to use the medication as somewhat of a crutch for a few days until the alcohol and the anti-anxiety drugs were out of my body.

You should not swap alcohol for illegal drugs. That is counterproductive. You are decreasing the damage to one part of your body and increasing the damage to another part of your body. If you think you need prescription medications for depression or other issues, go to a doctor and let this professional decide what is best for you. If you have been on an alcohol binge and want to get off cold turkey, you may want to ask your doctor if you need some medication for the first few days.

Keep your doctor informed and involved during your withdrawal from alcohol if you are a heavy drinker and especially if you are sick from alcohol abuse. Make double sure that you tell your doctor how much you have been drinking and for how long. And, do not lie to this person. I feel that this is very, very important.

The doctor can decide if you are a candidate for delirium tremens. "DT's" is a condition people develop when they have consumed lots of alcohol for an extended period of time and suddenly stop. DT's can kill you, and it is an ugly way to go.

If you continually do bad things to your body when you know that what you are doing is bad, then you are killing yourself. You can tell your body to quit doing something bad and your mind could make your body quit. You cannot tell your body to get well when it is very sick and expect good things to happen every time.

GET TO KNOW YOURSELF

Get past the first day and look at yourself in the mirror. Congratulate yourself. Tell yourself that you made it through today without drinking and you will definitely get through tomorrow even better than today. Sounds silly, but you will learn to appreciate your own accomplishments if you spend just a minute or two confessing to the mirror. Do not speak out loud. Look at your eyes in the mirror and hold the gaze for a moment. You cannot lie to yourself in the mirror.

Every day, the mirror reflects a more friendly face. You are being true to yourself. After a few weeks, you will begin to admire the image in the mirror. No kidding. You will think of the fact that you have quit and you will give yourself a little nod. That usually happens after you have had a good day or a good previous day. Even after a bad day, as long as you did not drink you have reason to feel good. You quit and you won.

After a time, you will know that there is no turning back to the way you were. You and others close to you admire this new person far too much for you to turn away from the progress you have made. Each new acquaintance does not need to know the way you were. You are not starting over with a different set of friends, but you are also not advertising the fact that you once were a heavy drinker.

Do not forget the way you looked and felt when you were drinking. Try to remember the stupidest thing you ever did when you were under the influence. That was you and you did do that. Remember it, but keep that person hidden forever. You must not go back to being that person.

You want everyone else to forget your actions when you were drinking, but you need to remember as if it were yesterday. You must look back and see your actions. You have to see how your actions affected others and how they possibly injured people you care about.

GUARD AGAINST FAILURE

If you have a friend or two who are unruly when they get drunk, you may need to reconsider how much you should associate with them. You do not have to give up on them, but you must make sure their careless actions do not jeopardize your success or your future. They could be the type who would get drunk and tease you about your sobriety. They might try to coax you into just one drink. "Just one drink" is what you promised that nice person in the mirror you were not going to do.

When I tried other programs to stop drinking and failed, I felt absolutely awful for quite a long time. I had failed and I could not take it back. All the progress, all the praise from family and friends, all that effort was for nothing. Gone were the smiles on the faces of people I love. It is truly a sickening, sorry feeling. I am a grown man from a tough background, but I cried myself to sleep both times I failed. I will not have that feeling again. I will not do that. I have quit.

When I stopped drinking in the past and failed, I did not have the proper attitude in my own head. I was not properly motivated, so I was never totally committed to quitting alcohol. I was lying to myself and others but I really could not see that. Give this book a few days of effort to settle in to your mind. Reread chapters four through eight a couple of times when you have dried out a few days.

When you make alcohol irrelevant as I have, you have lived through your last hangover. You have thrown up a hundred dollars worth of very good whiskey for the last time. After a month or two of sobriety, take a smell of your formerly favorite alcoholic beverage. Stinks, doesn't it? You have quit.

You will read some of this and shake your head, but it worked for me. I had failed with other methods because I would not go through with all the guidelines set forth in some of the other programs. You have my entire program in your hands. You must simply choose not to drink. Just get your own head on straight and you are on your way.

I feel certain that if you accept the mindset I am suggesting in this book, you can definitely give up alcohol altogether and not drastically change your entire way of living. You are simply changing one aspect of it. You are not drinking alcohol. You have quit.

SAY IT AGAIN

In summary, I feel that these are the major success points you must keep in mind to make sure you quit drinking and stay quit:

*   You must convince yourself that you will quit and then do it. There can be no wavering. No beer in the back room. No vodka miniature on the way to work. If you do, you have lied to yourself.

*   Do not punish yourself. You may have done some ugly things in the past, but you are about to do lots of fixing.

*   If you must go into rehab, go in peace. If you require medication, take it only as it is prescribed and do not drink any alcohol. When you get out, do what you have been told to do and do not drink alcohol. You are one day closer to success.

*   Do not lie to your health care professional (doctor, nurse, psychologist, etc.). Do not even think of telling a lie to your health care professional.

*   Remember who you were. Be proud of who you are.

*   Watch your own back. Do not allow anyone to coerce you into having a drink.

* Be quietly proud of your sobriety. There is no need to verbally advertise the fact that you have quit. They already know.

* You must commit yourself to your own sobriety. You must recommit to yourself every day.

* Your positive attitude is essential to your success. There is absolutely no way that you can quit drinking alcohol if you do not have a positive attitude.

CHAPTER SIX

LIVING SOBER

Once again, much of the conviction I impart in this chapter comes from personal experiences and what I have learned from other people who have had issues with alcohol. This is not information from a doctor or psychologist. These are my personal opinions and information I have gathered from people who have been there.

OK, so you quit. This is your first day without alcohol. Now what? Your friends say they want to go for a beer after work. Holy cow. I am going to look stupid without a drink in my hand. What do you do? You go and enjoy yourself. You can not sit around the rest of your life, worrying if someone will convince you to go back to alcohol. Cheerfully accept the offer to go and have coffee or soft drinks.

Do not precondition your participation in the get together. You are there, but you are not drinking. Do not announce anything, just go and have a good time. Be just as you always have been, but without an alcoholic beverage in your hand. Non-alcohol beer or club soda will do just fine.

"You're not drinking?" You can simply say that you are on the wagon for awhile. Or that your doctor said you should lay off liquor for awhile. No need to say that it is a permanent change because that invites questions. Order something and change the subject. If someone persists, you could say that you are going to take a break from liquor for a while. As far as you are concerned, it is no big deal.

You should not have to tell a lie to justify your decision to quit drinking. If this is the situation, you may need to take a look at your collection of friends. No one will be noticing your club soda after the second round. You should not move the conversation to your change of lifestyle. If it is brought up by others, deal with it in a way that this change is really unimportant.

Do not walk into work on Monday morning and announce your lifestyle change to eternal sobriety. That will cause a stir. They will find out soon enough what you have done and also if you are serious. They will be able to tell right away that you have quit by the way you look and the way you smell. Your face is not puffy, your eyes are not glazed and your breath does not linger with them after you leave the room. I cannot tell you how bad someone's breath can be after their first cup of coffee mixes with that rum from last night's Pina Coladas. After six years of total sobriety, you too can become pious.

ARE YOU CONFIDENT IN YOUR CONFIDANT?

If I learned one thing from my mother-in-law, it is that people will talk. Whether it is good or bad largely depends on your actions. If you give people ammunition they will use it. You must make sure you only provide them with the good stuff. They can no longer say you came to work today stinking of gin. Coworkers can say that you were late, but they may think that you probably had a good reason because you are not drinking anymore. You can now call in sick and people will believe you.

Confide only as much as you want everyone to know. Spare the details unless you feel that it is important that this person knows more information than you want others to know. Watch out, or everyone will know.

Once again, sometimes people just cannot stop themselves. If they find out something that they think no one else knows, the temptation could be just too great. They may feel very remorseful after they have satisfied the inquiring minds, but now everyone knows exactly why you quit.

As a former hourly employee who came up through the ranks, I can tell you from experience that it is extremely difficult to keep juicy gossip to yourself even if the gossip is about yourself. Be careful what you say to whom about quitting alcohol. Stating that you have quit drinking suggests that you have a habit at the very least.

Rumors will abound if you are a high profile person in the company. This is to be expected. Smile when someone says they heard X from Y about your former drinking problem. "Why is it important to them? I am doing what I want to do at this time." I feel that is absolutely all you need to say. Let it go. Do not go to Y and make a statement of any type. Do not tell one person one reason you have quit and someone else a different story.

If you choose, you could just tell everyone the whole truth. At this time in your life, you feel the need to quit using alcohol in any form and that is the end of the story. That is just another variation of the same "I quit because it was time" statement. There should be no explanations unless you feel that people deserve one. If you feel that comfortable with those around you at work, go ahead and tell them your story. I would really think this one over a couple of times before I completely exposed myself.

PERSONALLY SOBER

It is life as usual at home. The only difference is that you are now sober all the time. Your spouse or significant other should already know why you quit, so there is no requirement to explain your new circumstance. They should continue their normal activities unless they are always overindulging. If your mate is constantly drunk, sooner or later there will probably be a problem in your relationship. You will start feeling better and better about yourself and sad for your mate. There may be a confrontation coming in your future.

If your mate is a social drinker but sometimes gets drunk, then your penance is to make sure they have a happy and devoted designated driver. Goodness knows, they probably did it for you. Go to the liquor store for them and smile at yourself in the mirror. You have quit. You do not need anything in the entire store for yourself.

If you are in a social situation and your mate begins to brag about the fact that you have quit, do not embellish their accounts of your success or the way you were. Just shrug your shoulders and say it is not a big deal. You have simply quit drinking. Then shut up and let someone else change the subject.

You want your mate to be a part of your success. If you love your companion you will want to show that your change in lifestyle should only enhance your relationship. They may become concerned that you are planning more than one change in your life. You must eliminate that concern. Thank them for working with you on this issue.

The longer you do not drink, the less anyone will consider it an issue. You will be shocked at how quickly your sobriety will not even be mentioned. You are now the rock of the group. You drive them home. They do not want to mention it to make sure you do not start back and they will have to drive drunk. Sound silly? It is a fact of life.

Children at home could be a delicate situation. You absolutely can never lie to your children about anything because they will find the truth. They already know much more than you think. Your children will notice immediately that something is different even if it is days or weeks before they say something. Do not ignore their direct or indirect inquiries regarding your change of life.

Tell your children the truth when they ask why you are not drinking. Just don't go into details. Tell them it was time for you to quit drinking and that is the end of the story. They will want to know that everything is OK between you and them; they want to be sure nothing is going to change between you and them. Tell them it is just going to get better and let them know you still love them. It is just time for you to quit drinking alcohol.

Communication between you and your children should improve as you continue to be sober all the time. As you are an adult and a parent, your kids have enough trouble focusing on what you are saying without the added variable of your liquor breath. They will probably have more respect for your opinion because it is no longer given while you are slurring your words.

Tell your parents and other relatives not to make a big deal over the fact you quit. The less said to and by immediate family and in-laws, the better. Just tell them all to let it go. You quit. So what? Once again, it will be a topic for a short period of time or as long as you want it to be part of the family dialogue. Let them know that you have not changed, you just quit drinking.

Now everyone who maters to you knows that you have quit. You cannot go back on your commitment.

CHAPTER SEVEN

MOTIVATION

WHY YOU ARE QUITTING?

What is motivating you to quit drinking? Are you afraid of what you have become? Are you concerned of what you may become? Are you sick? Have you been given an ultimatum by a boss, judge or loved one? The fact that you have decided to quit is the single most important thing you could do for yourself and those who love you.

Several years ago when I was in a group therapy session, a couple told us they would give their young daughter some cash and send her into the local convenience store to buy them a carton of milk. They were both afraid they would go to the cooler and buy beer. They were both outwardly horrified that they would possibly start drinking again. They had failed so many times that they actually feared convenience stores.

Those people may have a real need to ingest alcohol or they may think they have a great need. They made it through four sessions and were absent the rest of the times I attended. I assume they failed in their attempt to stay sober. I thought from the first time I heard their story they were feeding off each other's negative emotions. I feel they were waiting for something to happen that would give them an excuse to get drunk and fall off the wagon.

These people described no motivating force in their commitment to stay sober. It was a halfhearted commitment at best. Their motivation seemed to be their fear of losing their children because of their alcohol abuse. They swore they had never taken illegal drugs and were only beer drinkers. Their need for beer had ruined their lives and the lives of their children.

You can not let that happen to you. You must motivate yourself to the point that there is nothing that can make you go back to drinking. You must succeed. Success is permanent abstinence from alcohol.

You cannot partially quit drinking. "Partially" and "quit" do not fit together in a sentence. You must quit all the way and stay quit. One glass of wine is a total failure on your part. You do not get up tomorrow and start over again on your quest for sobriety. You must stay away from alcohol today until you go to sleep tonight. You can worry about tomorrow when it arrives. There is no room for one glass of wine today. Have one beer or mixed drink and you have failed yourself, your family and everyone else who is counting on you to succeed.

There should be no other motivation necessary except that you have guaranteed yourself that you will not drink alcohol. Who else do you have to please? If you stop drinking, you have pleased everyone including yourself. You must go forward with the pride and poise of a person who is now in total control of their own destiny.

You must remember how it was when you were drinking. If you got drunk in bars, I would bet that someone has laughed in your face because of the sorry state you were in and you do not even remember it. If you do recall such an event, how could you possibly allow yourself to go back? You are moving yourself into a new level in life. You are no longer vulnerable to jokes about how you behave or have behaved.

The time may come when people you know will tell stories of what stupid or dastardly things you did while you were drunk. They will probably expect you to laugh at yourself along with them. Smile and file that story away as another motivation to stay sober and never allow any new stories about you to become a part of this person's memory files. You must make sure you outlive the stories of the way you were before you quit. They will fade away if you do not add new material.

I can tell you from personal experience that getting back on the wagon gets tougher each time you fall off. That within itself should be motivation enough to fight any desire to have a drink. I have told you of my failures. If you fail too many times, you may give up and accept hangovers as a way of life. Failure would mean that you would go back to being the principal character in bar stories.

NEGATIVE COMMENTS, POSITIVE MOTIVATION

I was sitting in a hotel bar in Fort Lauderdale a few months before I was fired, trying to figure out how I lost a contract I had been working on that week. It was late and I was one of about five customers left in the old horseshoe bar. I was telling my tale to a young bartender, who was pretending to be interested in my story. Without expecting an answer, I asked the bartender how in the world I could have missed out on the contract.

From across the bar, an older man looked over to us, raised his glass and quietly said "Because you're a drunk. You're drunk right now and you will always be that way." He had already paid his bill, so he took his last sip, saluted me with his empty glass and walked out of the bar toward his room. The bartender and I just looked at each other as he walked through the door. I shrugged my shoulders and ordered a night cap. I have often remembered that night and my actions. I accepted what the man had said as a fact and ordered another whiskey. If I am tempted to take a drink, I think about that rude old man and smile. He is a part of my motivation to quit drinking alcohol forever.

I have been told by several people that I will not remain away from alcohol. People I have known for years have laughed in my face when I told them I have quit drinking. Some of those people were my friends and some are no longer my friends.

Hurtful words can be powerful motivators. If someone tells you they do not believe that you will stay sober, you could simply cast your eyes downward and wait for the moment to end. If you do that, you have not quit and you are kidding yourself or you realize that this person is a royal jackass and it is easier on you legally and financially to let them say what they want and get out of your face. Today, I usually just look at them with a knowing smile and say nothing. I have quit and I will prove it if it takes me a lifetime.

I firmly believe that negative feedback can make a person as determined to win as positive reinforcement.

When someone says in a smart way that I am not going to make it sober, I become even more determined. All I have to do to prove them wrong is stay sober. Game over. I quit.

I HAVE QUIT

I WILL STAY SOBER

You must make a vow to yourself that this is the time for success. You must swear to yourself that you have quit and will not go back to being the butt of jokes. I do not think it matters one bit what oath you give to others. What matters is what you know in your own heart. You may not think you can stay sober the first few days or weeks. You must push yourself to maintain the course. You must make a vow to yourself that you will stay sober. You cannot lie to yourself.

You are not a drunk. You may have been there but you have moved past that part of your life. We have already discussed that from the moment you quit, you must never again consider yourself a drunk. You must not even consider failure as a possibility. You are now sober and functioning as a responsible adult. You absolutely cannot go back to where you were in life.

My principal motivator is what I have to lose. Quit and I have a fighting chance. Go back to alcohol and I have lost everything. I believe I had already lost some of the respect my wife and kids had for me. I told myself that I would do whatever that was required to make them forget my previous actions.

You have every reason to succeed. You must convince yourself that you will stick with this program until alcohol is no longer a consideration in your life. You can do it if you properly motivate yourself. Just simply tell yourself under your breath that you have done it. You have quit.

CHAPTER EIGHT

ATTITUDE

If you enter this new phase of your life without the proper attitude, you already have two strikes against you. Your attitude helps guide your level of commitment. Your commitment is something you are devoted to; something you have to work on for it to be successful. You cannot be devoted to a goal if you do not personally feel that you can succeed. Without a positive attitude, there is no positive commitment.

Your attitude comes from within your own mind and the actions of those around you. If you are receiving positive reinforcement, you should feel more positive regarding your personal situation. If you have people close to you who are not supporting you in your efforts to quit drinking, they are affecting your attitude in a positive or negative way.

If someone has your best interests as their primary concern, they should be wholeheartedly supporting your decision to quit drinking. They should be telling you that you are doing the right thing. They should be thrilled with the sober person they are seeing. If they are not outwardly optimistic that you will be successful, your opinion of and your association with that person may need to be revisited.

Your attitude can be your biggest asset or your worst enemy in your efforts to quit drinking or anything else you plan to do that is important. My attitude was poor when I first contemplated quitting alcohol. I was not sure I could do it with or without help from others. As I gathered more information regarding liver disease and found a primary physician with a positive attitude, my personal opinion of my chances of quitting began to grow.

TIME CAN IMPROVE YOUR ATTITUDE

During the first few days of sobriety, I did not give up on my commitment, so my attitude had a chance to change for the better. I thought at the time I was paying a temporary penance, but every day without alcohol improved my attitude regarding the possibility that I could indeed quit drinking forever. I was starting to believe I could do what appeared to be a monumental task in the beginning. I was now consciously making plans without alcohol as part of the equation and I was starting to believe I could quit. my attitude grew more positive.

As your confidence in your ability to quit grows, your overall attitude should improve. You are progressing, you know it and it shows. You have given this new lifestyle a chance and it is working. Your personal opinion of your chances for success is improving and your attitude is now changing for the better.

People close to you will begin to notice your new and improved attitude as much as the fact that you have quit drinking. They will see that you present yourself as more confident and they should like the change. You now appear to be more in control of your actions and emotions. Your newly found positive attitude is now an asset. People close to you will marvel at your new attitude long after they stop noticing that you do not drink anymore.

You can tell when a person you meet has a positive attitude. You can see it in their eyes and the way they carry themselves. They seem more pleasant and have a sense of calmness about them. They are not as afraid of tomorrow as you are right now. If you are serious about quitting, you are wary of the future and you know it. The longer you have been sober, the better your attitude will be, and fear will be less and less a part of your life.

You should feel a more positive change beginning in your attitude not many days after you quit drinking. On occasions, I felt almost exhilarated because I had made a week, two weeks and so on without a drink. You will not believe it until it happens to you, but it will happen. I thought that it was really stupid of me at first, but I grew to like the rush of confidence. It is actually feels like a burst of euphoria. My doctor says that it is an enzyme being released into your system. I say it is a happy moment in my soul for my body still being alive.

Success breeds confidence and confidence breeds a more positive attitude. It is almost a wonderful circle of life. Failure tears down confidence, and that deteriorates your attitude. Make your commitment to quit drinking, and as you live with your commitment a few days, you will feel your attitude start to improve. You will be amazed at yourself in a few weeks.

Your confidence will begin to build at a rapid rate and your attitude will be at an incredible high. You have quit, you know it and so does everyone else.

CHAPTER NINE

COMMITMENT

In order to win at anything worthwhile, you must commit to that endeavor. You can win at playing the slot machines or buying a Lottery, but the odds are against success on a regular basis. If you buy a Lottery ticket when the prize is $20 million but you choose not to buy a ticket when the prize is $3 million, you are not a committed Lottery player. Commitment means that you are striving for success every day of your life.

In my opinion, not being afraid to live sober in an environment that includes alcohol really shows a commitment to sobriety. Being afraid of alcohol shows a lack of total commitment. You are not committed because you are not sure in your own mind that you can accomplish the goal of total sobriety. If you cannot make that commitment, you are in trouble and could use some more work on your attitude and motivation.

I know several bartenders who have had issues with alcohol in their personal lives, but they made a commitment to themselves to quit drinking and were successful in their efforts. They now serve liquor every work day but do not drink a drop. They do not even consider drinking alcohol as something they would want to do anymore.

They have committed themselves to sobriety and have developed the proper attitude. They see it, smell it, serve it, hold full bottles of liquor in their hands; but they no longer have the desire to get drunk or even have a social drink because they know the eventuality of that action. They have witnessed failures by others who thought just one would not be a problem..

Commitment has already been indirectly discussed throughout this book. Telling yourself that you can do something and following through is making a personal commitment. It is a positive action within your mind.

Trusting in your own ability to quit drinking is a powerful commitment.

INVITATION

I was born into the Southern Baptist religion and have remained a member of the Baptist faith. You could look at this chapter of the book as the invitational hymn. This is the time when the music is softly playing as the pastor walks down in front of the congregation and asks who is ready to commit to this new life. Are you? Why should you?

If you use this book as your template for success and quit drinking right now, the results could be dramatic:

* You could regain the respect of your family.

* You could regain the respect of your friends.

* Your loved ones could be proud of you. Maybe more than ever.

* Your self respect could skyrocket.

* You may save your marriage or another valuable relationship.

* You could save your job.

* You may be able to improve your job situation as a sober person.

* You may save your own life.

If you have a drinking problem and do not quit, the results could be catastrophic:

* At this moment, you are probably as loved and respected by your family as you ever will be. Your life will most probably be downhill from here.

* You are probably at the height of your popularity among your friends and colleagues. As your drinking problem becomes worse, you will probably see less of them because they may not want to be a part of your downfall.

* You are probably as successful as you ever will be in your entire lifetime. When you start fading in business, your decline could be fast and dramatic. If you think I'm kidding, reread Chapter Two.

* Your mate will know that this is the best they can expect from you as a person. Everything gets worse after today. This is the best it will get for your mate.

* You are as healthy as you ever will be. Nothing about your health will dramatically improve as long as you continue to assault your body with constant barrages of alcohol.

* You could be preparing yourself for a very painful death. Everyone you love and who love you will also be in pain.

AND THE ANSWER IS

You now have the good news and the bad news. There is no doubt that you can quit by committing to a life of sobriety. That is the good news. The bad news is that you can continue drinking and possibly destroy your entire life. This commitment to staying sober can be easier than you think. Millions around the world have quit drinking. I feel that the ones who went back to a life of alcohol were not steadfastly committed to their goals.

You must be motivated to quit drinking. Your family, your boss, your mate or you personally may have seen the need for you to quit drinking alcohol forever. It is now up to you to motivate yourself. Use every external support mechanism you feel will help you to stay motivated and committed to a long life of happiness and sobriety. However, the bottom line is you and your attitude, commitment and personal motivation to quit drinking alcohol.

A positive attitude is an absolute necessity for your efforts to be successful. You must tell yourself you can succeed and mean it before you can accomplish anything in your life. Others have said you cannot win by supporting the possibility of failure. A half-hearted effort will lead to failure and sadness for you as well as those who love you.

It is your decision. Quit drinking or stay drunk. Choose your fate.

CHAPTER TEN

"SCARED SOBER"

LIVING WITH LIVER DISEASE

If you have been told by a medical professional that you do not have liver disease but you drink alcohol every day, it may be wise to read this chapter just to familiarize yourself with what could happen if you continue to abuse alcohol.

Earlier in this book I stated that I would offer you what information I have gathered regarding liver problems. Once again, I am not a physician or a practitioner of any type of medicine. The person to give you medical advice is your doctor. My information comes from my experiences and what doctors have told me regarding my personal liver problem, observations from people with liver problems, and the internet. If my information conflicts with your doctor, listen to your doctor.

On two different occasions a few years ago I was told that my liver enzyme tests indicated problems. Both times, I stopped drinking for a few weeks until the numbers fell to within acceptable limits. I knew I should quit then, but I stopped just long enough to satisfy my doctor and to placate my wife. If I had quit at that time, I would not have this horrible problem today.

I will try to explain to you some of the awful possibilities you could face if you drink too much for a long period of time. I may not have the definitions absolutely correct, but hopefully my interpretation will give you an idea as to the severity of the situation. If your body warns you, listen.

THE REALITY OF CIRRHOSIS,

BY SOMEONE WHO HAS IT

So you have been diagnosed with cirrhosis. In my opinion, the first thing you must know is that you must never drink alcohol again as long as you live. Everything else in your mind should be secondary to making absolutely sure that you do not take another drink of alcohol, ever. Pray, scream, sleep, curse; do whatever you have to do to stay away from alcohol. Your life is at stake.

If you continue to drink, you could die an ugly death sooner rather that later. It's just that simple. I have lived with cirrhosis for over seven years by not drinking, eating right, taking lots of vitamins and doing as much exercise as I am physically able to do. I also elevated my attitude from feeling sorry for myself to looking at life as a gift.

Your head is probably still spinning around with all the information being thrown your way. I will add to the mix, but I will give you simple definitions and what I did to beat even my most optimistic mortality estimate. I hope this information helps you understand what you can do to extend your own life. As you probably know by now, there is no medicine or treatment on the market to cure liver disease other than a transplant.

PORTAL HYPERTENSION

Other than death, one of the most feared medical conditions resulting from cirrhosis is portal hypertension. It brings on several other maladies that could cause serious if not fatal problems if they are not treated as absolutely soon as they are identified. I will give you a short layman's explanation of portal hypertension and related conditions.

As I understand it, portal hypertension occurs when blood is trying to get back to the heart through the portal vein and takes its normal route to the liver for purification. However, the pathway through the liver could become blocked because of damage to the liver. The blood is under pressure from the heart and tries to find different ways to get back to the heart. The blood redirects itself, usually through the small vessels found in the esophagus or those in the rectum. These blood vessels could become swollen and rupture.

Esophageal varices is very dangerous. If you are a heavy drinker and begin to lose blood from your mouth, I would strongly suggest that you go to the nearest emergency room as quickly as possible by whatever safe and legal method of transportation you can find in a hurry. I have been told that a person usually has one hour of consciousness left after they start vigorously coughing or vomiting blood. Check with your doctor for a proper explanation of this complication of liver disease. Varices is usually a direct result of portal hypertension so the description of both maladies are intertwined.

In my case, beta blockers did a great job in bringing my portal hypertension under control. The medication also helped control the varices before they ruptured. Propranolol, a beta blocker prescribed for me, acts to lower my overall blood pressure and pulse. My doctor wanted my pulse rate down to the low 60's. I was very sleepy during the early days of beta blocker treatment, but we finally reached an adjusted level where I could function and my pulse stayed where my doctor thought was best for me. If you smoke and have varices, I feel that you are only making the situation worse because you are introducing an additional irritant into the already critically inflamed internal area.

There are a few effective procedures used by doctors to help control the different types of varices. Hopefully, you are a long way from having an intimate knowledge of these procedures. If you want to know more about them now, check with your doctor or go online. I do not think that any of them are fool proof as far as being a permanent fix. The doctors are probably most interested in stopping the blood if there is an eruption and then trying to prevent a recurrence.

ASCITES

Another very serious complication of portal hypertension is the presence of ascites. When you have cirrhosis, your body tends to retain salt and fluids. As this fluid builds, it starts leaking through your liver and other organs, and collects in your abdominal cavity. That fluid is called ascites. I was having congestive heart failure as a result of the ascites in my abdomen as it caused pressure on my lungs. I would have panic attacks because I was out of breath from the slightest exertion and my heart would begin to pound uncontrollably. One problem was aggravating another problem.

I was eating when I was not hungry just to satisfy my wife. I would often throw up the food because I was so stuffed after only a small meal. The doctor told me when my treatment started that the pressure of the abdominal fluid was killing my appetite and causing me to vomit the food to reduce the pressure in my abdomen. Therefore, I had become malnourished because of the ascites and only wanted to consume more liquids.

Diuretics worked quite well in reducing the fluids in my entire body. They are now part of my body maintenance program. I begin to retain water quickly if I miss only one day of my scheduled medication. I have been taking my water pills religiously every day for years and have learned to eat well on a salt restricted diet.

ENCEPHALOPATHY

Hepatic encephalopathy occurs when poison cannot be filtered from your blood stream by your liver. The toxins affect your brain function and could cause you to become confused to the point that you change your behavior and could even cause death. Allowing a good doctor to monitor your blood tests and direct your treatment could help control encephalopathy. If you do the right things after you have been diagnosed with cirrhosis and portal hypertension, you may never have to deal with this disorder.

There are several methods of treatment that doctors can utilize to help remove poisons from your body and lessen the severity of hepatic encephalopathy. If necessary, they can regulate your intake of protein if you begin to show signs of this disorder. They can give you lactulose, which works as a laxative to take some of the toxins out of your system. Enemas can be useful in some cases.

Falling off the wagon can cause encephalopathy to quickly present itself. If you go on a binge, you may think you just have a bad hangover, but go to your doctor immediately after you get sober. Your condition could be far worse than you imagine. Your body may now be full of more poisons than just alcohol.

I have spent many nights in bars, listening to people argue points that I think they had no idea what they were talking about. They spoke with such positive assurance that they would almost convince me that they were authorities on the particular subject. After enough whiskey, I have been known to join in on the discussion. Having learned more about encephalopathy, I now believe that we were speaking with authority because our brains were full of poisons and alcohol.

If you get any type of infection, this could also bring on encephalopathy in a short period of time. If you visit a general practitioner or an emergency room doctor who is not familiar with your medical history, make sure they know that you have liver disease before they prescribe any medications to you. Certain medications can cause encephalopathy to present itself in liver disease patients.

INFECTIONS

A problem that could develop from either ascites or varices is infection. Your body and your doctor have a real problem fighting infection if you have cirrhosis. Many antibiotics manufactured to fight various infections are metabolized in the liver. If the liver is already damaged, these antibiotics could do further damage and impede recovery.

Bacterial infections are especially deadly to you as a liver disease patient. Bacterial peritonitis is a very dangerous complication for patients with ascites. Some researchers say that when the fluid begins to leak into the abdominal cavity from the liver and the bowels, it carries bacteria with it. The bacteria can infect the organs from inside the abdominal cavity and a whole body infection can develop very quickly.

You must be very proactive in your efforts to bring portal hypertension under control to help your doctor make sure the other complications are avoided. One complication could bring on far worse conditions. In my opinion, you and your doctor are not curing a single one of the complications of cirrhosis we have discussed in this chapter. You are putting a bandage on the condition until it gets better, so you can live a long and happy life. That is really all you and your doctor can do until medical science develops a better treatment or a cure for this dreaded condition.

PANCREATITIS

Alcohol is one of the leading causes of acute pancreatitis. You could end up on life support as a result of an inflamed pancreas. Social drinking over a number of years and then going on a binge can bring on an attack. People who abused alcohol over a long period of time could feel sick for a few days before experiencing severe pain and blood pressure issues when they have an inflamed pancreas. Go online or speak to your doctor if you need more specific details on this condition

As I have stated earlier, if you are a heavy drinker or even a social drinker and have been on a binge, do not assume that the way you feel is because of a bad hangover. It could be any number of maladies that could do permanent damage to your body. If you are a heavy drinker and feel bad for several days after a binge, get yourself to a doctor and tell the truth as to what you have been doing to yourself.

KEEP YOUR EYES OPEN

There are several other conditions associated with cirrhosis, but these are the ones I fear the most. If you want to know more in a hurry, you can go online and search for complications of cirrhosis. Personally, I would deal with the big ones first and work my way down to the ones that won't kill you. Solve the big problems first and some of the little ones may just go away.

Please remember that despite all these dire possibilities, life is not all gloom and doom. You are still here and there are some very good doctors and researchers out there working to make us healthy. Every day is a victory. It is never, ever too late to quit drinking and fight for your own life. I have decided that doctors, nurses and technicians really do enjoy saving lives and watching their patients do well. If you give it your best and acknowledge that they are doing the same, you may be surprised how well you do in your recovery.

CHAPTER ELEVEN

HELP YOURSELF

Once again, the information I provide you in this chapter is what I as a layman have found out from doctors, fellow patients and the internet. Please conduct your own searches on the information I provide in this chapter. Best of all, ask your medical specialist.

Among the stupidest plans I have ever made was to take a full dose of ibuprofen or acetaminophen at least twice each day to help prevent hangovers, relieve the pain I experience from osteoarthritis and at the same time not upset my stomach with aspirin. The consensus in the medical community is that I made a monumental mistake. These two pain relievers and alcohol in large proportions are widely considered to be lethal to the human liver.

I totally disregarded the warnings on the labels regarding consumption of these products and drinking more than three alcoholic drinks per day. I was taking the maximum dosage at least twice a day and chasing the pills with about a six pack of beer. I kept up this practice for about a dozen years, so I may have done some significant damage to my liver this way as well. It might be a good idea for you to read the warning labels better than I did.

If you have consumed alcohol for any period of time, I strongly believe it is a good idea to have periodic blood tests that focus on how your liver is functioning. These tests are commonly referred to as a liver function panel or liver enzyme tests. The enzymes they will be testing for have long names that are hard to spell, so I will use abbreviations. Your doctor will most probably use the same method to identify the tests. If you want to have all the exact names, ask your doctor's nurse or go online. I learned quite a bit about blood work as an Army medic. That is why I tried to avoid giving my doctor the ammunition to recommend that I quit drinking.

Two of the most common blood tests run to detect liver damage are referred to as AST and ALT. They are both good indicators, but I have been told that the ALT is more accurate in identifying liver damage. The ALT enzyme is mostly found in the liver and is usually found in the blood after damage to the liver. If your ALT number is in the high range, the possibilities are good that you have had some type of liver damage.

The AST enzyme is released by your body when you have liver damage, but also when you have a heart attack or some other damaged muscle. Therefore, I have been told that the ideal number for AST should be in the middle of the scale. A low number could mean there is liver damage, where a high number could mean heart or muscle damage. In my opinion, believe the ALT test and hope for a mid-range AST score.

Bilirubin is created as a byproduct of the red blood cells breaking down in your bloodstream, which is part of the normal body process. When bilirubin cannot be dumped from your body through your liver, you could begin to turn yellow as the bilirubin levels rise in your bloodstream. The total bilirubin test will indicate the amount of this waste that is in your bloodstream.

Information from other tests is also beneficial to your doctor. Albumin and total protein tests help your doctor know if your body is producing enough blood proteins to maintain your muscles and organ tissues. The doctor also needs to know if you have too much protein in your body. Always, always go have blood work done if your doctor suspects there is a problem. You may be delighted to find that there is no problem and you have time to eliminate bad habits before they become dangerous to your health.

VITAMINS

All my doctors agree that vitamins are very important to your body's well being. However, there is some disagreement as to the best method of acquiring these necessary vitamins. My family doctor says to eat healthy and take a multivitamin every day. My VA doctor says that taking a vitamin pill simply results in expensive urine.

I believe that I would rather pass unneeded vitamins in my urine than have a deficiency of something that could help me. If your body does not need everything in a vitamin supplement, it would stand to reason that the excess would be passed through the kidneys. If the vitamins will not hurt you, they must be helping or being passed from your system.

Almost everyone agrees that alcohol depletes the B vitamins from your system. When I first began seeing her, my family doctor told me to start taking large supplemental doses of thiamine and folic acid in addition to a multivitamin. She eliminated the additional B vitamins after about four months but insisted that I continue the multiple vitamins.

If you feel that you consume enough of all the proper foods to give yourself all the vitamins and minerals you need to get or stay healthy, then save your money and avoid the multiple vitamins. Check with your doctor if you want some additional advice on the subject. Personally, I take a generic multivitamin every morning and eat lots of fruits during the day instead of desserts.

MILK THISTLE

The jury is still out on the benefits of milk thistle, but the market is booming for the product. You may purchase milk thistle at a grocery store, health food store, flea market, online or many other outlets as a single product or blended with other herbs. Many people believe that this herb has been a real benefit in their efforts to obtain or maintain good liver health. Some researchers agree and some are not so sure.

When I first became concerned that I was drinking too much and may be damaging my body, I went to a health food store and asked if they had any herbal products that would promote liver health. The "advisor" showed me about a dozen different packages promoting milk thistle as the main ingredient. He said that some of his regular customers were very pleased with their personal results after using the herb over a period of time. I was not convinced because of the fact that it was not a prescribed medication and may conflict with my doctor's treatments.

My advisor reminded me that milk thistle is a plant. He stated that the milk thistle root grows in the ground. Can ingesting plants really affect the human body enough to make a great change? Marijuana is a plant that is grown in the ground. Smoke marijuana and you really should not operate machinery. Eat it in brownies and you will want more chocolate. Think of what the opium poppy does when the chemicals found in the plant hit the blood stream. I got the point.

At my next appointment, I asked my doctor about milk thistle and the possible benefits. She shrugged her shoulders and said that the herb has been associated with liver treatment for only about 2,000 years, so it probably would not hurt to give it a try. I went online to get some more information and found that a large number of the articles on the subject also stated that milk thistle had been considered a liver health aid since the time of Christ's birth. I could not find a single article that denied human benefit from the use of this product.

Milk thistle was originally found in the countries around the Mediterranian Sea. The people of that part of the world somehow came to believe that this herb

helped rid the liver of toxins and it has been popular
ever since. These were some pretty smart people and
apparently came to this conclusion without the aid of
microscopes and modern empirical studies. I went
back to the health food store and bought a large supply
of the ultra, super duper, mega formula and have been
doing pretty well ever since.

Many people believe that milk thistle can actually cure
liver disease. I am not so sure of that, since I have been
taking the product for several years but I still show
cirrhosis on my CT scans and sonograms. It may have
helped in the stabilization of my liver, but it has not
healed me, even though I am taking the mega formula.

Milk thistle is also taken by people who want to
continue drinking alcohol and at the same time make
sure they do not do damage to their liver. There is
strong belief worldwide that this product will do just
that. I have my doubts that any herb or combination of
herbs can prevent liver damage if the level of alcohol
consumption is heavy and sustained over a long period
of time.

Perhaps you should check with your doctor to see if milk thistle might have interactions with your prescription medications or any other health issues you may have. If you have allergies, you should definitely check with your doctor before taking this herb. Diabetics should check with their doctors first before taking milk thistle.

My opinion is that if it will not hurt you, it probably will help you.

ARTICHOKE LEAF

Yes. Artichoke. If you eat every part of the artichoke, you could get pretty sick. However, according to many researchers, if you eat only the artichoke leaf or an extract from it, you can help keep your liver healthy or improve your chances of survival if you have liver disease. The ancient Romans are generally credited with this discovery exactly two thousand years ago. These people must have been pretty heavy drinkers in the day or they were really smart. Maybe they were smart enough to know what was good for people who drank too much.

The artichoke leaf reportedly contains a substance called cynarin, which is said to increase liver function. The artichoke supposedly stimulates the flow of bile from the liver. You can laugh if you want, but millions of artichoke tablets have been sold to people who are concerned about their liver health.

LECITHIN

According to studies, the nutrient choline is found in lecithin. Lecithin is found in the health food store. I have read that Veterans Affairs has taken part in studies regarding the possible benefits of lecithin/choline for liver patients. I cannot understand the findings, but I take triple-strength lecithin as a dietary supplement every day. It is sold in a soft gel and is not expensive.

Lecithin is supposed to keep fat from binding inside the human body and helps prevent fatty liver. Fatty liver leads to cirrhosis. Thus, it stands to reason that lecithin should help prevent cirrhosis. Lecithin is supposed to actually aid the body in repairing damage done to the liver by alcohol.

The liver will try to repair itself and many researchers around the world believe that lecithin will definitely assist the organ in its healing efforts. If it only helps to expel fat from the liver, it has been well worth what little you pay for it as a dietary supplement.

WHY SUPPLEMENTS AND NOT PRESCRIPTION MEDICINES?

My doctors are not aware of prescription medications that even claim to help remove fat from the liver or increase liver function. At the very least, I feel that I am trying to give my liver a fighting chance at survival. I am not doing further damage to my liver and I am helping it with dietary supplements, or I think I am helping it with these supplements. Either way, it helps me to sleep at night.

Lots of people around the world feel that milk thistle helps your liver if you do or do not have liver damage. Many people, including researchers, feel the same about lecithin and artichoke. I feel that all these products could actually help people who continue to drink in moderation if their livers are not badly damaged.

According to the medical professionals I trust, prescription medications are just not out there to cure cirrhosis or associated liver problems. You can slow down your pulse to help control portal hypertension. You can take diuretics to remove salt and water from your body to prevent swelling and other serious complications. But I do not know of a single prescription medication that claims to help restore normal liver function.

DIET

Many doctors and dietitians believe that you can eat your way out of liver problems. I have found that you can actually dine very well on a liver patient's diet. Several books are available on the subject and they make good sense.

Lots of green vegetables and foods low in fat are featured in most liver diets. Restricting salt within the diet is also very important. I have actually gained muscle since I have been following the regimen set by my doctor. You will not go hungry on my diet and after a period of time you do not miss the heavy salting of food.

We still eat out, but I am now much more specific in how I order my food. Fast food is a thing of the past, except for fruits and salads with dressing on the side. It is really not that difficult to modify your eating habits if you give it some thought and effort. I definitely feel better when I am on the liver friendly diet.

CHAPTER TWELVE

LAST WORD

As you have probably guessed, I left out some of the gory details from my life of self abuse. I told you a couple of times that some of the things you did and went through should be kept hidden and remembered only by you. That goes for me as well. You did not need to hear about all the places I fell or got sick. That has probably happened to all of us who drank too much.

I have moved forward and you need to move forward. It was what it was, and it is what it is. You can move forward, quietly proud of your accomplishments. In my opinion, you do not have to go around shouting that you are a drunk and a useless reprobate. You are not. At least, not anymore.

Please remember some of my points for success:

* You must convince yourself that you have quit and then do it. There can be no wavering. No beer in the back room. No vodka miniature on the way to work. If you do, you have just lied to yourself.

* Do not punish yourself. You may have done some ugly things in the past, but you are about to do lots of fixing.

* If you have to go to rehab, go in peace. If you require medication, take it as it is prescribed and do not drink alcohol. When you get out, do what you have been told to do and do not drink alcohol. You are one day closer to success.

* Do not lie to your health professional (doctor, nurse, psychologist, etc.). Do not even think about telling a lie to your health professional.

* Remember who you were. Be proud of who you are.

* Watch your own back. Do not allow anyone to coerce you into having a drink.

* Be quietly proud of your sobriety. There is no need for you to verbally advertise the fact that you have quit drinking. They already know.

* You must commit yourself to your own sobriety. You must recommit to yourself every day.

* Your positive attitude is essential to your success. There is absolutely no way that you can quit drinking alcohol if you do not have a positive attitude.

Thank you for taking this time to read my humble recipe for success over alcohol. I think it is simple enough to grasp but for it to work, you must totally commit yourself to the idea that you will quit drinking alcohol.

Please let me say again, you are the key to your own sobriety. You can quit drinking alcohol. Please give it a chance and you will find that you can quit forever and be happy. No one else can do this for you. Make everyone who loves you proud of you and be proud of yourself. Quit drinking.

HOW I QUIT DRINKING ALCOHOL WITHOUT GROUP THERAPY

ABOUT THE AUTHOR

Don has been a marketing executive in the marine industry for over 30 years. He currently lives in Jacksonville, Florida with his wife and three cats. He has two children: a attorney and an artist.

www.ingramcontent.com/pod-product-compliance
Lightning Source LLC
Chambersburg PA
CBHW072141280526
45788CB00002B/730